Cleaning Up the Sea

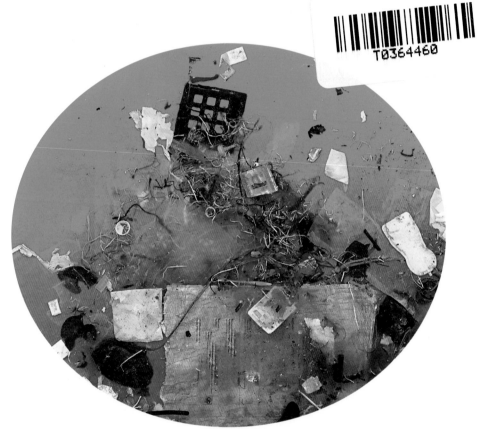

Written by Catherine Baker

Collins

The plastic problem

The blue seas are full
of plastic rubbish.

First, plastic gets into a river. Then the river sweeps the plastic out to the sea.

Sea currents push the plastic onto beaches.
It can get wound around living things.

Plastic collects in floating rubbish dumps, way out at sea.

Each day, plastic in the sea gets pounded down into little bits.

Living things like sea birds eat the plastic, and it may poison them.

Solving the problem

Humans have found clever ways to clean up plastic, like this collecting pool.

This floating boom traps dirt and plastic in a river.

boom

This clean-up shark sucks up plastic and brings it back to land.

This big shrimp keeps a seaport clean by scooping up rubbish and dirt.

Beach clean-ups stop plastic getting into the sea. Children and adults all enjoy joining in.

Way out at sea, this fishing boat tries to help by scooping up plastic rubbish.

Here, men are collecting stray plastic nets.

Boats can reach the big rubbish dumps out at sea.

They trail a long boom to trap the plastic and bring it back to land.

What can you do?

First, get rid of plastic rubbish in the right way! Then it will stay clear of rivers and seas.

If you are near the coast, join
a beach clean-up.

That way, you can help rescue the sea
from plastic.

Keeping the sea clean

🐾 Review: After reading 🐾

Use your assessment from hearing the children read to choose any GPCs, words or tricky words that need additional practice.

Read 1: Decoding

- Challenge the children to look at these words in context and think of another word or phrase that has a similar meaning.

  page 14 **way** (*far, a long way*)   page 17 **trail** (*drag, drop*)   page 18 **clear of** (*away from*)

- Ask the children to read words that contain specific sounds on these pages. Can they identify the graphemes?

  page 3 /ow/ (**out**)   page 6 /ai/ (**day**)   page 7 /ee/ (**eat, sea**)

  page 12 /oi/ (**enjoy, joining**)

- Ask pairs of children to pick a double page spread and take it in turns to read each page aloud. Say: Try to blend the words in your head silently first, before reading your page aloud fluently.

Read 2: Prosody

- Turn to pages 4 and 5, and model reading the pages in the voice of a television presenter who is warning viewers about the problems.
- Ask the children to work in groups to practise reading the pages like a television presenter, to draw the viewers in.
- Remind them to think about tone, which words to emphasise, and pace.

Read 3: Comprehension

- Encourage the children to share their experiences of pollution, and where they've seen it or what they've done about it.
- Ask the children what they have learnt about cleaning up the sea. Suggest that they list all the different ways that the cleaning can be done. (e.g. *booms, machines, people: clean-ups, fishermen collecting it*)
- Ask the children some questions and give them time to look for the answer.
  For example: What can poison living things? (*plastic*, page 7) What machines clear plastic? (*clean-up shark and big shrimp*, pages 10–11)
  - o Ask the children to think of their own What? Where? Who? or Why? question. Tell them they must be able to point to a page for the answer.

  - o Let the children ask and answer each other's questions. If necessary, ask for clarification by saying: Can you tell me which page shows that it's right?

- Turn to pages 22 and 23. Can the children explain how the things in each photo help with cleaning up the sea? Which of the inventions in the book do they like best, and why?